995

THE 1989 SAN FRANCISCO BAY EARTHQUAKE

PORTRAITS OF TRAGEDY AND COURAGE

PROJECT EDITOR
Angela Rinaldi

DESIGN
Cylvia Santillan

COPY EDITING
Clark Stevens

CAPTIONS
Kevin Roderick

PRODUCTION
M'Liss Bouayad, Katherine Anderson

TYPESETTING
Grette Stamnas, Gwen Torges

ISBN 0-9619095-1-X

Published by Los Angeles Times, Times Mirror Square, Los Angeles, California, 90053.

COVER PHOTO
The cover photo which depicts the collapse of the Bay Bridge was taken by Lori Shepler.

THE 1989 SAN FRANCISCO BAY EARTHQUAKE

PORTRAITS OF TRAGEDY AND COURAGE

By the staff of the Los Angeles Times

PHOTO EDITOR
Larry Armstrong

TEXT EDITOR
Craig Turner

On the Monday after the quake, many commuters left home early to beat the gridlock expected as throngs returned to work. Traffic here on the Golden Gate bridge into San Francisco is backed up well before dawn. But by 8 a.m., traffic was flowing more smoothly than on a typical Monday. The bridge authority suspended the usual $2 toll in the aftermath of the quake.

Photographer:
J. Albert Diaz

CONTENTS

Clock on the landmark Ferry
Building at the San Francisco
Embarcadero stopped when the
quake struck. Nearby high-rise
buildings in the financial district
escaped serious damage.

Photographer:
Jayne Kamin-Oncea

''It wasn't really the Big One.''

Philip Hager

To live in California is to live with earthquakes. The same geologic forces that created the state's unsurpassed beauty—the jagged Sierra Nevada, the spectacular beaches, the glistening sweep of San Francisco Bay—have left California stitched with underground faults. The most famous of these—the San Andreas—has become synonymous with the state.

Scientists have repeatedly warned in recent years that a major earthquake—something like the estimated 8.3 magnitude quake that destroyed San Francisco in 1906—is due along the San Andreas over the next half-century or so. It could come, they say, anytime along the fault, which runs nearly the length of the state.

Californians even have a term for this projected quake. They call it the Big One.

But unlike hurricanes, tornadoes and other violent acts of nature, earthquakes come without warning. In quake country, one may be generally prepared for a temblor, but when it occurs it is inevitably a surprise.

On October 17, 1989, people in the San Francisco Bay Area were enjoying the kind of warm afternoon typical of autumn. A party atmosphere reigned over much of the region, for the World Series featured a historic confrontation of cross-bay rivals, the San Francisco Giants and the Oakland Athletics.

At 5:04 p.m., as Candlestick Park filled for the third game of the series, the San Andreas shifted. The friction point was 11 miles beneath the Earth's surface in Santa Cruz County, about 50 miles south of San Francisco. The coast side of the fault—the Pacific Plate in geologist's terms—slipped 5½ feet to the north and 3¾ feet toward the surface. The inland side—the North American Plate—slipped southward.

The whole thing lasted 15 seconds, but it left a 100-mile swath of misery unmatched by a natural disaster in California in 83 years. Buildings cracked and burned. A freeway collapsed on itself. A 50-foot section of the San Francisco-Oakland Bay Bridge crashed to the deck below. In the tiny town of Loma Prieta in the Santa Cruz mountains, a fissure 6 feet wide, 15 feet deep and 1,000 feet long opened in the earth, slashing the driveway in front of Freda and John Tranberger's home.

At Candlestick Park, a buoyant crowd of about 62,000 was awaiting the first pitch, just 30 minutes away. When the temblor struck, Mark Dandrige, a security guard, saw the stadium tower sway and the

President Bush flew past the crippled section of the Bay Bridge on his inspection tour of quake damage. Workers are making preparations before the fallen piece of the upper deck can be lowered onto a barge.

Photographer:
Bernie Boston

luxury box seats begin to shake. "Oh, God help us!" he said aloud. A fan, Marsha Blanche, had a thought that undoubtedly was shared by thousands of parents: "Who'd raise my kids?" The game was canceled and the World Series would not resume for 10 days.

On a Bay Area Rapid Transit train riding beneath San Francisco Bay, passenger James Herron Zamora felt the wheels bounce on the tracks and thought he would be sick. "People next to me were crying," he recalled. "One woman started praying in Spanish."

In his apartment in the stylish Marina district of San Francisco, David Doiron was asleep on the couch when the quake struck, knocking plaster off the walls and hurling the contents of shelves to the floor. Doiron fled quickly—and vowed not to return until the building was declared structurally sound. "My apartment is a disaster," he said ruefully.

Dozens died instantly. Others suffocated beneath the cascade of broken concrete that had been the Cypress Street viaduct of the Nimitz Freeway in Oakland.

Many of those who escaped death would lose all their possessions. Others would wait days in agony for building inspectors to examine their homes, leaving behind one of three colored notices—green for OK to resume occupancy, yellow for all right to retrieve belongings, or red, meaning tagged for demolition.

There were heroes, too. Heading home on the Nimitz Freeway, police officer Al Wong saw the roadway collapse, stopped his car, grabbed his first-aid kit and instructed onlookers to go get ladders, ropes and more help. Firefighters worked frantically to free a group of nurses trapped in a van, managing to save three. Surgeon James Betts, working with paramedics, labored three hours under floodlights to amputate a child's leg and free him from the collapse.

The hopscotch pattern of destruction spared the vast majority of the region's 5 million residents, leaving them to face only traffic jams and other inconveniences. They were the lucky ones—and most of them knew it.

When it was over, the scientists were there. They counted the aftershocks—about 4,000 in the first few days, many strong enough to serve as a fearful reminder of the event itself. They warned of the possibility of more aftershocks, perhaps all the way until Christmas.

And they assigned a magnitude of 7.1.

"We should really consider this earthquake a kind of warning shot," said Paul Reisenberg, a seismologist for the U.S. Geological Survey, "As horrible as it was, it wasn't really the Big One."

Californians live with earthquakes.

First section of upper Bay Bridge
roadway—weighing 100 tons—is
lowered onto a barge. Engineers
feared doing further damage to the
53-year-old bridge. But after 4½
days spent preparing to lift off the
section, the 300-foot-tall crane did
the job smoothly and safely in five
minutes. Downtown Oakland is in
the background.

Photographer:
Ken Lubas

Jean Cleverly lost almost all she
owns when the quake destroyed
her Marina District apartment. Here
she sits across the street.

Photographer:
John Carey

Overview of San Francisco's Marina District, scene of most of the city's quake damage. The area was built on fill—used to reclaim a former cove on San Francisco Bay—after the 1906 earthquake. A World's Fair was held there in 1915. The quake's tremors reacted with the fill to weaken the ground, leading to extensive damage even 75 miles from the epicenter.

Photographer:
Jim Mendenhall

The Marina Collapses

Dan Morain and Victor F. Zonana

From inside her Marina District home and office, Lee Phillips knew it was not the usual earthquake when the brick facade of her building went crashing down onto Divisadero Street.

If the San Francisco architect needed any further evidence, she got it when she scrambled toward the door. "I couldn't walk down the hallway," she recalled. "I fell down five times."

When Phillips finally made it outside, she was dumbstruck by the devastation around her. Several buildings on her block had "pancaked," she said. Others were tilted precariously or had been hoisted from their foundations and into the street. The smell of natural gas filled the air.

About 20 minutes later, smoke began to spill out of the windows of the collapsed apartment building at Divisadero and Beach Streets. Then came the fire. The gas-fed inferno raged for 14 hours and consumed one-third of a block. In the days after the quake, the intersection would become known to San Franciscans as "Ground Zero."

But Phillips, who lived a half a block from Ground Zero, counted herself among the lucky. Around San Francisco, a dozen people did not survive to tell their stories. The youngest to die was a 3-month-old baby, crushed when the apartment building he lived in collapsed around him.

All over the city, power failed, sirens wailed and shattered glass and broken bricks covered the streets. Survivors, dazed and jolted, poured from homes and office buildings, clustering around battery-operated radios, swapping stories or waiting for pay phones.

Mayor Art Agnos raced from Game 3 of the World Series at Candlestick Park to direct the response from an emergency command post several blocks from City Hall. The quake struck just half an hour before the scheduled first pitch, terrifying many of the 62,000 fans who had packed the ballpark.

"We're having an earth . . ." reported a voice on ABC-TV's pre-game show, as screens went blank across the country.

"The upper deck was absolutely shaking; the light stanchions were blowing back and forth," said Suzyn Waldman.

The most serious cases of damage at the park were a six-inch crack that ran the length of one stairway on the upper deck and the separation of a support stress joint at the very top of the upper deck. Steel bolts fell on fans, but there were no serious injuries.

Ten days later, when the series resumed, many fans wore hard hats.

In the first panicked moments after the quake, people throughout the city could barely believe they had survived.

"All I was thinking of was being buried alive," said Marcus Williams, 26, who ran from the federal courthouse. People all around him were screaming. Mark Dunlop was playing racquetball in the Embarcadero YMCA. As ceiling plaster began to fall around him, he ran down the street in his gym clothes. "I really thought I was going to die," he said.

"I saw the sidewalk moving," said Charles Thomas, a bus driver standing stunned outside his disabled bus.

Five people did die, at 6th and Bluxome streets, buried when a brick wall fell onto a parking lot. Office workers wailed as firefighters and young men tried to pull people to safety.

"I saw the building coming down," Cliff Bailey said. He was in his car and pulled forward to avoid the cascading masonry. Then he stopped and tried to rescue people from the rubble. "I saw two bodies," he said.

Like hundreds of thousands of commuters, Jeff Darling was stranded in San Francisco, left to wonder about the fate of his family across the Bay in Berkeley. "Answer! Damn it!" he shouted into a downtown pay phone that rang unanswered at his home. Thirty seconds later, he dropped the receiver and began to cry. "I've got to know," he said. "I've got to know. What happened?"

"I wanted nothing more than to see my babies. To see their faces," said Jean Chastang, 31. She was at work at Children's Hospital in San Francisco. In Oakland, her children, ages 7 and 11, were too frightened to go into their home after school. They were waiting on the front porch when an aunt finally arrived for them at 9:30 that night.

Beth and Dick Lundin, conventioners from Newport Beach, were relaxing in the lobby bar of the Hyatt Regency when a four-ton metal sculpture nearby began to sway. They feared it would come off its massive reinforced concrete stand.

"I thought it was going to stop, then it got worse," Lundin said. That night, the couple caught a few winks of sleep on the first-floor ballroom with table cloths for blankets and 1,500 other hotel guests as roommates.

Skyscrapers survived—but not without giving their occupants gut-wrenching rides.

"People were fighting to get under desks," said David Balague, who was on the 14th floor of the Bank of America building. "It felt like we were swinging through space," added Betty Brookes, who was on the 46th floor of 101 California Street.

As the sun set, there was almost no wind. Black smoke hung above the waterfront, as the inferno blazed out of control in the Marina.

Emergency workers, trying to move onlookers back, shouted that the smoke was toxic. Toxic or not, the smoke burned one's lungs. Paramedics did not want to guess at the number of people who might have been caught inside.

"It's a nightmare," an elderly woman said, watching the fire, uncertain whether she would be allowed to return to her apartment a few doors away.

The earthquake had snapped water lines so, for a time, there was not enough water to fight the fire. The Fire Department sailed the Phoenix, its 35-year-old fireboat, onto the Marina. For 14 hours, the Phoenix pumped 10,000 gallons of bay water a minute into the apartments. Days later, the remains of one person were found.

At 7 p.m. on Oct. 17, neighbors and rescue workers heard the cries for help of a man and woman trapped in a second-story apartment at Cervantes and Fillmore streets in the Marina. Rescuers, in a futile attempt to get oxygen to the couple, hacked at the wreckage with a chain saw.

The following day, when workers were able to get through, they found the bodies of Diane Laufer, 40, and Paul J. Harris, 48, embracing under a door frame.

Horst Schwandt, a chef at Trader Vic's who had lived in the Marina for 23 years, stood across from the demolished 30-unit building. Like a generation of San Franciscans, Schwandt knew he lived on a fault line. It was something he and most other natives made jokes about.

"We took it lightly before," Schwandt said. "It was funny. Now it's not."

▲

Unlike 1906, when huge fires swept the city, the only big fire was in a block of apartments in the Marina District. Several buildings were destroyed.

Photographer:
Anne Dowie

▶

A Marina District house shaken off its foundation and into the street. Most of the more than 250 San Francisco buildings that suffered serious damage were here. Most of the neighborhood's streets would have to be torn up after the quake to repair natural gas lines.

Photographer:
Jim Mendenhall

Red Cross volunteer Sheila Peck takes a break on Friday, the third day after the quake, and tries to keep warm. Temperatures dropped in the Bay Area, adding to the misery of victims and volunteers. She was working in the Marina District.

Photographer:
J. Albert Diaz

Aerial view of destroyed building in the Marina District. At least one floor of apartments simply disappeared beneath the collapsed rubble.

Photographer:
Jim Mendenhall

Another collapsed building in the Marina District.

Photographer:
Bob Carey

On some Marina District streets, sidewalks buckled and buildings were tossed several feet.

Photographer:
J. Albert Diaz

This building in the Marina District wobbled off its moorings and just settled. The neighborhood is on top of a filled-in portion of San Francisco Bay.

Photographer:
Larry Davis

▲

A body is carried from the rubble
of a Marina District apartment
building.

Photographer:
J. Albert Diaz

An aerial view of collapsed Marina District building.

Photographer:
Jim Mendenhall

Rescue dogs were used to help look for survivors in collapsed Marina District buildings. This building was on Divisadero Street.

Photographer:
Larry Davis

Baseball legend Joe DiMaggio, a longtime resident of the Marina District, waits with other displaced residents for information and clearance to enter their homes. A green card gave permission to go home. Yellow allowed a brief visit to take stock of the damage. A red card marked the building for demolition.

Photographer:
J. Albert Diaz

Resident of the Marina District hurries to salvage as much as he can during the short period he was allowed into his building. Inspectors restricted the time as a safety measure, but were widely criticized by residents.

Photographer:
J. Albert Diaz

▲

Volunteers, such as Harry Herwick,
helped move the belongings of
elderly Marina District residents
who were forced from their homes.
The building facade shows cracks
from the quake. Structure was
posted unsafe by city inspectors.

Photographer:
J. Albert Diaz

In the Marina District, apartments
that had been on upper floors often
sagged nearly to the ground. Some
residents of upper floors searched
for pets and prized possessions by
clambering over debris.

Photographer:
Tom Kelsey

Peter Flores tries to look inside his apartment. The Marina District building was left teetering by the quake.

Photographer:
J. Albert Diaz

▼

_____

Sometimes legally and sometimes not, Marina District residents scampered to recover family treasures, pets, clothing, photos—anything they could find—from the rubble of their apartments and homes. Here an unidentified man retrieves belongings from what used to be a second-story apartment.

Photographer:
Bob Durell

▲

Paul Coviello carries personal effects out of the canted doorway of a once-grand Marina District building. He was allowed a quick trip in to retrieve property.

Photographer:
Bob Carey

◗

Marina District residents were forced to flee the neighborhood with what they could carry. Some stayed with friends or family. Others checked into motels or went to Red Cross evacuation centers.

Photographer:
Larry Davis

Quake victims Mary and A.J. Hales
huddle in blankets outside a Red
Cross shelter in San Francisco.

Photographer:
Bob Durell

▲

Earthmover rips apart building that was already destroyed by the quake. Quake left a fickle mark on the Marina District, toppling some buildings but leaving others standing.

Photographer:
Bob Durell

▶

Kim Bruninga survived the quake on the fourth floor of the apartment building in the background. Here she and friend Doug McKenie remove some belongings, including a quake "Survivor Pak."

Photographer:
Tom Kelsey

●

Bob Richards, left, and Louis Rivera
try to pry loose a garage door in the
Marina District. They were installing
support beams trying to keep the
building from collapsing.

Photographer:
Tom Kelsey

A house plant is pulled intact from
the wreckage of one Marina District
building leveled by the dozers.

Photographer:
Tom Kelsey

Crowd gathers to watch demolition
of a Marina District apartment
building where two people died.

Photographer:
Anne Dowie

▲

Marsha Drayer had to wait until the bulldozer knocked down her building before she could retrieve any possessions. Here she salvages a few cherished clothes.

Photographer:
Tom Kelsey

●

Sherman Chen sorts through the debris of his Marina District dwelling after it was demolished on orders of city inspectors.

Photographer:
Bob Carey

An idle bulldozer used to knock
down quake-damaged buildings
frames a Marina District structure.
This building, heavily damaged, is
typical of the style in the district.

Photographer:
Tom Kelsey

The displaced of the Marina District gather to hear Mayor Agnos promise relief aid, but also warn that residents must stay out of dangerously damaged buildings.

Photographer:
Larry Davis

Woman watches giant earthmover grab pieces of a Marina District apartment building that was ordered demolished. Behind her, workers had painted "searched" on another damaged building to indicate that no victims were inside.

Photographer:
Tom Kelsey

▲

Other than the Marina District, the
hardest hit areas of San Francisco
were south of Market Street and in
the Mission District. Here a San
Francisco policeman walks through
the rubble of a collapsed South of
Market building.

Photographer:
Larry Davis

View of deadly avalanche of bricks and rubble that tumbled off a building in the South of Market area.

Photographer:
Anne Dowie

San Francisco Mayor Art Agnos on
the scene in the Marina District, a
week after the quake. Officials were
making the fateful decisions on
which buildings to tear down.

Photographer:
Bob Carey

Scavengers search the rubble of
another building in San Francisco.

Photographer:
Tom Kelsey

Bricks hurtling off a building
buried this car. Six people
died in the rubble of the building.

Photographer:
Anne Dowie

Prayers were said for the quake
victims at Sunday morning service
in San Francisco.

Photographer:
J. Albert Diaz

▲

Along most the Nimitz, the lower
deck held. But near the north end
of the quake zone, workers inspect
the gash where both decks of the
elevated freeway buckled and fell to
the ground. In the first hours after
the quake, the Oakland Fire Department had only a few ladders tall
enough to reach motorists who
were stranded atop the freeway.

Photographer:
Gary Friedman

TRAGEDY
The Nimitz Freeway

Andrea Ford and Tracy Wilkinson

When the earth began to shake, the double-decked section of the Nimitz Freeway began undulating like a crepe-paper streamer. Then it snapped.

Tons of concrete that had formed more than a mile-long span of the upper deck of the freeway's Cypress Street viaduct slammed with unimaginable force onto the lower level. Cars below were crushed to a height of less than a foot. Others were crumpled like aluminum cans. On the upper deck, cars and tractor rigs were tossed into the air and dropped onto the adjacent side streets.

"The freeway just started rustling, waving . . . rocking," said truck driver Harrison Brown, whose rig was hurled against falling concrete slabs. "Imagine . . . all of a sudden the road in front of you just drops. All around, these people screaming and hollering."

The freeway, a section of Interstate 880, runs along Oakland's inner harbor, then cuts inland above Cypress Street through a predominantly poor neighborhood of housing projects and aging Victorian homes to the eastern approach to the Bay Bridge. It is a major commuter route. But, mercifully, traffic was uncharacteristically light that afternoon, partly because the third game of the World Series had inspired people to leave work early.

Nevertheless, at least 41 people would die in the single most deadly disaster of the October 17 Bay Area earthquake.

Those killed on the Nimitz represented the diverse economic, social and ethnic strata that so typify the Bay Area: Donna Jantina Marsden, 36, a hospital administrator who had been making her usual afternoon commute in a shuttle van with six co-workers from UC San Francisco; Gary Watson, 54, a delivery truck driver transporting wine from the Napa Valley; Vinh Phu, 32, an immigrant from Vietnam who was driving his three children home from school (the children survived); Rosalpina Hurtado, 25, a refugee from Nicaragua accompanying two sisters to their night job as cleaning women.

There were many more lucky ones, like Darrell McDaniel—shaken and injured but alive.

As the ground pitched, McDaniel's pickup truck slammed against the top guardrail before flipping in somersaults. When the truck came to rest, McDaniel climbed out and watched as dazed, bleeding, screaming people struggled to free themselves from twisted metal and fractured concrete.

"It was like a science fiction movie, like those old San Francisco

●

Pillars lying at an angle used to hold
up the upper deck of the Cypress
section of the Nimitz Freeway. The
fallen pillars separated from the
support columns in the quake and
toppled outward, allowing a mile-
and-a quarter stretch of the upper
deck to collapse. Though the quake
occurred during the afternoon traffic peak, fewer commuters than
usual were on the road, perhaps
because of the World Series.

Photographer:
Bob Durell

quake movies,'' thought McDaniel, a bookkeeper. ''But this time I was in it.

''You could hear the cars on the level underneath exploding (popping as they were crushed), people hollering, asking for help,'' he said. ''Cars were falling, slapping down onto the pavement that kept moving out from under them. There were creases in the highway. It was buckling, snapping in half, falling in pieces . . . People were just lying all over the streets.''

Screams, moans and the acrid smell of burning fuel filled the air.

Two blocks away, William McElroy, a 52-year-old West Oakland boilermaker, stood at his back door staring transfixed at the collapsed freeway. He had driven home over the same stretch of freeway only minutes before.

As dust billowed skyward and black smoke from burning cars jetted from crevices between the two freeway decks, McElroy rushed to the site to offer help.

Others from his neighborhood and passers-by had the same instinct. What they found was a scene of incredible, almost surreal, horror.

Stunned survivors were milling about on the shattered top deck. Some of the injured were bleeding badly. As yet, no police or firefighters were on the scene.

''We're going to get you out of here,'' McElroy shouted as he mobilized an ad hoc rescue team.

Two forklifts borrowed from a nearby business were used to bash through a fence that formed a barrier along the freeway and had prevented McElroy and others from reaching the victims. Then, the forklifts raised wooden pallets to the top of the wreckage so people could be lowered to safety. Residents ran back to their homes for ladders and ropes and other gear.

Elsewhere on the freeway, similar efforts were under way.

Don Rich, a 47-year-old sculptor who came upon the collapsed freeway as he drove toward his studio, got out of his car and climbed a partially shattered support pillar, going hand-over-hand up the twisted and exposed reinforcement bars.

''I crawled up and looked into the spaces between the layers; there was dust everywhere,'' Rich said. ''I climbed up inside and got a few people out. I carried one man halfway down and realized he was dead.''

In the frantic hours that followed, fire trucks, ambulances, police cars and other emergency vehicles swarmed to the scene and launched what would become a round-the-clock, sometimes gruesome search for survivors.

Toiling through one of the most torturous rescues that first night, Dr. James Betts worked for more than three hours to free Julio Berumen, a 6-year-old trapped in a car with his sister, Cathy, his mother, Petra Berumen, and a family friend, Yolanda Orozco.

The two adults were found dead. Cathy, seriously injured, could be pried from the car. But Julio was pinned into the wreckage by the weight of Orozco's body.

To reach the boy, Betts first had to slither 20 yards on his belly through a two-foot crawl space. Then, Betts had to cut through Orozco's body and amputate the boy's right leg to free him.

"I hope I'm never involved in something like this ever again," an exhausted Betts said as Julio recovered at Children's Hospital of Oakland.

As rescuers worked feverishly into the night, Caltrans engineers surveyed the damage with a growing sense of dread. Forty-four 90-foot sections of the upper freeway, each weighing 500 tons, had fallen onto the lower deck. Pointing to a normal daily traffic flow of 195,000 cars on the Nimitz Freeway, engineers and officials feared more than 250 people had been killed. That estimate would prove high, thanks to the lighter than usual traffic flow.

In the days that followed the quake, eager rescue crews were increasingly daunted by the tedious and dangerous mission of searching the wreckage for victims, even as aftershocks and settling further weakened the viaduct. The slow, methodic pace of the rescue frustrated and angered some volunteers who believed that if they could reach victims sooner, more would be found alive.

Assistant Fire Chief Al Sigwart, one of the handful of commanders in charge of the Nimitz operations, was constantly forced to weigh the need to move quickly against the dangers that the precarious structure posed to workers. It was a balancing act that led to bitter disputes among some volunteers.

"I was worried that the entire freeway could fall to the ground," Sigwart said.

"We were not going to risk known life for unkown life," said California Transportation Department engineer Bob Travis.

As specially trained dogs sniffed the rubble for survivors, workers used spray paint to mark spots where cars or bodies had been detected. Sophisticated sensing equipment would be brought in and concrete-

Jackknifed truck left stranded atop the crumpled, fallen deck of the Nimitz.

Photographer:
Gary Friedman

crunching tractors would cut through pieces of roadway to open passages for rescuers.

When a car was found, workers would use the "jaws of life," powerful metal cutters, to remove the roof and pull out the bodies.

The scenes inside the catacombed structure were eerie. One volunteer crawling through the rubble spotted a couple sitting in the front seat of their trapped white Honda Prelude, much of which was intact. The man's and woman's eyes were closed but they bore no obvious injuries.

After three days of futile searching, a Caltrans engineer inspecting one section of the collapsed freeway peered into an opening and spotted the last known survivor: Buck Helm. His rescue invigorated the crews deployed at the Nimitz site, but it was a short-lived respite.

A week after the quake, Caltrans engineers, signaling an end to any hope that additional survivors might be found, began dismantling part of the freeway. Demolition of the collapsed Cypress viaduct was expected to cost $10 million and take a month or more to complete.

Long before rescue operations ended, debate raged over why the Nimitz Freeway was unable to withstand the quake. Caltrans officials disagreed publicly over whether the 32-year-old freeway had been adequately strengthened as part of a statewide retrofitting program.

Civil engineers from UC Berkeley and US San Diego, after a weeklong investigation, concluded that there had been cracking at the joints that connected the columns to the lower deck, allowing the upper roadway to fall on the lower lanes

Further investigation was under way.

Just northwest of the freeway collapse, the earthquake wrought an equally frightening but far less deadly piece of destruction on the Bay Bridge.

A 50-foot section of the bridge's upper roadway plunged onto the lower level, falling into the path of Oakland-bound commuters. Amazingly, only one person was killed—Anamafi K. Moala, 23, of Berkeley, who drove her car into the gap left by the collapsed section.

The 53-year-old bridge, a vital link between the East Bay and San Francisco, is normally traveled by close to half a million commuters daily. But as was the case on the Nimitz, traffic on the Bay Bridge that Tuesday afternoon was lighter than usual—thanks to the World Series.

Elsewhere in the East Bay, the quake left seemingly random pockets of devastation.

Alameda County reported that 350 people were injured and more than 2,500 were displaced and homeless; damage will total $1.5 billion. In addition to the ravaging of homes and six low-income hotels, Oakland lost use of its historic Catholic cathedral, several downtown department stores and even its landmark City Hall.

Sadly for Oakland, the quake hit at a time the city was undergoing something of a renaissance. Long considered the dowdy stepsister to the magical city across the bay, Oakland has recently seen millions of dollars poured into redevelopment of its downtown commercial district and waterfront.

"It's almost unbelievable that man could construct something . . . and that it could be so vulnerable to forces of nature," said Oakland Mayor Lionel Wilson. But he and other local leaders vowed that the city will recover.

"The tragedies we have suffered here in Oakland will strengthen our fellowship and pride in our city," Wilson said. "Oakland . . . will rebuild on that firm foundation."

Searchers atop the fallen section of Nimitz Freeway extricate a body from the debris. Many police and fire departments sent disaster crews to Oakland to observe the rescue efforts. Some also videotaped the reaction to the quake to help train crews back home.

Photographer:
Lori Shepler

On Campbell Street in Oakland, near the Nimitz bricks are cleared off a smashed car.

Photographer:
Gary Friedman

Code spray-painted on the pillar means workers located two victims—unfortunately, not alive—pinned beneath the fallen upper deck of the Nimitz Freeway. The code was used to speed the grim task of locating bodies, which would not be dug out of the rubble until later, sometimes days later.

Photographer:
Bob Durell

This Toyota was one of the cars trapped when the Nimitz upper deck collapsed in the quake.

Photographer:
Gary Friedman

A truck with little damage is hoisted off the Nimitz upper deck, two days after the quake.

Photographer:
Gary Friedman

Ruined house within sight of the Nimitz Freeway in west Oakland.

Photographer:
Jayne Kamin-Oncea

Heavy pieces of concrete, such as this one, fell with a boom as workers finally began to dismantle the collapsed freeway. This was near 9th Street in west Oakland.

Photographer:
Ken Lubas

▲

100-ton concrete columns dangle from the Nimitz wreckage. The columns had held up the upper deck.

Photographer:
Ken Lubas

►

View of the Nimitz Freeway after Caltrans crews had begun to dismantle sections that stood through the quake. Although they did not collapse, they began to show cracks several days after the quake, forcing evacuation of about 150 residents of a nearby low-income housing project.

Photographer:
Lori Shepler

Even a week after the quake, demolition continued late into the night. This is looking north from the BART station on 7th Street. The sound of falling debris could be heard for blocks around in the West Oakland neighborhood.

Photographer:
Ken Lubas

Crowd watches the demolition work
on a section of the Nimitz Freeway.

Photographer:
Lori Shepler

Early Thursday morning, less than
36 hours after the quake, two
California Highway Patrol officers
sit by as workers try to shore up a
damaged secton of the Nimitz. Support beams were installed to rein-
force the lower deck so that rescue
work could go on above. Settling
and the fear of new collapses forced
halts in the rescue efforts at several
times in the days after the quake.

Photographer:
Lori Shepler

▲

Overview of a piece of the Nimitz
shows how the pillars that sup-
ported the upper deck failed and
fell outward. The freeway seemed
to collapse in sections. In some sections, the upper deck collapsed to
within inches of the lower deck.
Some cars that were traveling on
the lower deck were squashed
beyond recognition.

Photographer:
Ken Lubas

THE MIRACLE MAN
Buck Helm

George Ramos and Ashley Dunn

He became the "miracle man" of the Bay Area earthquake, a burly, 57-year-old longshoremen's clerk who unbelieveably survived 90 hours in the pulverized remains of his Chevy Sprint before being pulled from the wreckage of the Nimitz Freeway.

Before the quake, Buck Helm was known around the Oakland docks as a stubborn and tough man who often spent weeknights in a rusting yellow van and who on weekends commuted 250 miles home to the mountain community of Weaverville to visit his four children and his ex-wife, Lorene.

Afterwards, they were writing a song about him, "The Ballad of Buck Helm."

Helm was headed away from work, bound for a night of poker in a card parlor north of Oakland at 5:04 p.m. on October 17. He was traveling the lower deck of the freeway when the top level crashed down.

A massive concrete beam had flattened the front end of his car. The driver's compartment was intact, but was only three feet high. Helm was upright in the driver's seat, twisted at an angle. He still had his seat belt on.

In the hours immediately after the quake, the section where Helm's car was trapped was searched at least four times by rescuers peering in from the outside. But no one saw him.

There he stayed until before dawn on Saturday, when a mechanized crane called a cherry picker elevated California Department of Transportation engineer Steve Whipple, 29, to a two-inch-high gap between the collapsed freeway decks.

Whipple shined his flashlight inside and saw, about 40 feet away, the back of Helm's head. Another dead body, he thought.

"Call it fate, but I decided to take one more look to see if there was another person (in the Sprint)," the bespectacled Whipple said. He had already jotted down a note that there was one or perhaps two dead in the car.

Then it happened: Helm slowly waved his left hand once.

"Someone's alive!" Whipple thought. "No, no, no, no. That's not possible."

Maybe it was just litter blowing through the beam of his flashlight, he thought. He looked again.

This time, it was unmistakable. Helm slowly rotated his head as if he were trying to turn toward the light. "When he did that, I knew he was alive."

Whipple excitedly called for other workers. Some were ready to smash a hole through the concrete above Helm and had to be restrained by other rescuers worried that the span might fall to the ground.

Transportation department engineer Bob Travis and other top-ranking officials at the scene cautiously considered the three different rescue routes to Helm.

Entering from above could bring the span down. Boring in from the west was deemed impractical. Digging in from the east seemed the best approach.

By 9:30 a.m., a 3-foot-by-2-foot hole had been carved in the side of the freeway and three rescuers crawled into the tomblike chamber.

Donald Stone, a rescue instructor from Tuolumne County, was the first to reach Helm.

"How's it going?" he asked.

Helm mumbled in a barely discernible voice: "What . . . is going on?"

Stone and Dan Mackay, a member of the Orange County Fire Department's heavy rescue team, which was flown in to assist in the Nimitz operation, used a hydraulic tool called the jaws of life to break open the car door. Oakland paramedic Diana Moore ministered to Helm while the rescue went on. At 11:32 a.m., Helm was lowered from the span and rushed to Oakland's Highland General Hospital.

He had suffered a fractured skull, three broken ribs, nerve damage to a leg and kidney problems from dehydration. While being treated, the thirsty Helm asked for a glass of milk.

While friends toasted Helm's good fortune, rescuers back at the fallen freeway were still shaking their heads.

"I just knew he was going to make it," said Greg Guyan of the California Division of Forestry. "He's a one hundred percenter. I just knew he was going to make it."

Helm's 35-year-old son, Greg, had a more direct explanation of why his father never gave up.

"He's an ornery old fart."

The family of Buck Helm, who survived the longest under the freeway
ruins—more than 90 hours. They
rushed to Oakland from the northern
California logging town of Weaverville after hearing that Helm, a ship-
ping clerk well-known on the East
Bay waterfront, had been found
alive.

Photographer:
Lori Shepler

Rescue workers remove one of the 41 bodies pulled from the Cypress section debris. This was Thursday, Oct. 19, the third day after the quake. Some workers had been on the scene almost the entire time.

Photographer:
Gary Friedman

View of fallen support pillars of Nimitz Freeway shows the power of the quake and the scale of the freeway damage. The giant 100-ton columns of concrete simply twisted away, shearing off from the steel reinforcing rods.

Photographer:
Jayne Kamin-Oncea

▲

A special service for Nimitz Freeway victims was held six days after the quake at Taylor Memorial United Methodist church in Oakland. Nearby, crews continued digging for bodies in the freeway rubble.

Photographer:
Jim Mendenhall

▲

A construction worker helps guide
a piece of Nimitz Freeway debris
during the search for victims trapped by the collapse. The laborious
process of picking away at chunks
of concrete and steel went on nearly a week before officials finally
stopped hoping to find survivors.

Photographer:
Jayne Kamin-Oncea

Three people died in the quake
debris of the Pacific Garden Mall,
the most heavily damaged section
of Santa Cruz. For a week after the
quake, merchants were not even
allowed in to retrieve their business
papers or the money left in cash
registers.

Photographer:
Anacleto Rapping

"Earthquake! Evacuate the Building"

Eleven miles beneath a steep canyon in the Santa Cruz Mountains, the earthquake began with a distant boom, the sound of the earth rupturing along the San Andreas Fault.

The epicenter of the earthquake was on a stretch of the fault that runs through a state park, only six miles northeast of Santa Cruz. The park, 10,000 acres of heavily wooded canyons threaded by streams, is a mountain wilderness that drops dramatically toward the ocean. While the only damage to the area—called the Forest of Nisene Marks State Park—was a few cracked redwood and oak trees and a handful of jagged fissures, neighboring communities were devastated.

After the earthquake much of the nation's attention was focused on the rubble-strewn Marina District in San Francisco and the collapsed upper deck of a section of the Nimitz Freeway in Oakland. But, proportionately, there was greater loss in smaller cities like Santa Cruz, Watsonville and Los Gatos, and in remote hamlets in the nearby mountains.

Homes grafted onto hillsides were wrenched off foundations and toppled down ravines. Historic 19th-century buildings collapsed. Hundreds of storefronts were reduced to shattered glass and splintered wood. Highways and roads buckled and were closed after huge landslides.

In Santa Cruz County, the earthquake caused more than $1.5 billion in damage, left more than 10,000 people at least temporarily homeless, destroyed hundreds of buildings and killed six people. The devastation was so widespread that as many as two-thirds of the older homes in Santa Cruz and neighboring Santa Clara counties sustained some damage.

The capricious destruction was manifested in myriad ways: a 6-foot wide, 15-foot deep, 1,000-foot-long gash opened in the earth, ripping through the front yard of John and Freda Tranbarger's Santa Cruz mountain home. For days the large fissure drew crowds of scientists and gawkers.

A pickup truck driven by Dale DeBenedetti struck three spooked horses that had bolted from a pasture as he drove along California 1 near Santa Cruz. He was killed when one horse crashed through his windshield.

Orchards in Watsonville shook and pitched, and, in a split-second, thousands of ripe Granny Smith apples dropped to the ground.

In a coffee company building on the Pacific Garden Mall in

●

downtown Santa Cruz, Robin Ortiz was killed, but her last act may have saved the lives of numerous others. Witnesses said Ortiz must have been the first in the building to feel the shaking, and she shouted: "Earthquake! Evacuate the building!" About 20 customers and workers made it out, but Ortiz, a supervisor at the coffee firm, was trapped inside when the roof collapsed.

In Santa Cruz County, residents have learned to live with disaster during the 1980's. In January, 1982, torrential rains flooded streams, creating giant mudslides that killed 22 people and destroyed dozens of homes. A year later, huge waves from a Pacific storm destroyed beachfront homes and restaurants and caused $30 million in damage. In July, 1985, wildfires swept through the mountains, burning about 15,000 acres.

Residents have been willing to endure the vagaries of nature in order to live on this idyllic strip of coastline, cut off from the rest of the world by the ocean on the west and the deep green mountains on the east. On Blue Ridge Drive, a steep, winding incline above the the mountain community of Boulder Creek, residents stay because they love the seclusion and the captivating vistas. They have endured mudslides, brush fires and many minor earthquakes; they have battled the elements and they have endured.

But this time, for many, nature finally prevailed. About 20 of the 50 homes on Blue Ridge Drive were destroyed or so badly damaged they were declared uninhabitable. After the earthquake,

Damage along a street inside the Pacific Garden Mall, a pedestrian and shopping district in downtown Santa Cruz. Several buildings dating from the 19th-century were damaged so extensively that authorities ordered their demolition.

Photographer:
Anacleto Rapping

Robert Buonosera, 41, stood beside his home, once a 1930's-style redwood bungalow overlooking a wooded canyon, now a pile of lumber and shattered glass. He recalled how he had just settled down to watch the third game of the World Series when he heard a loud rumble and felt the shaking.

"I started walking toward the door," he said. "It was shaking so much I couldn't run in a straight line. I fell down three or four times trying to get away."

Outside, on the ground, he looked back. "I heard timbers snapping—the house was slowly leaning forward. And then all of a sudden it crashed down."

Numerous others along a ridge at the top of the street also watched as their homes collapsed or slid down hillsides. While in San Francisco the lowlands felt the full force of the earthquake, here it savaged the ridge houses grafted along the hillsides. Despite the destruction, many vowed to rebuild if they could obtain the necessary permits.

"I love the area," Buonosera said. "I was willing to put up with the risk and I still am . . . . It's absolutely beautiful here, one of the most beautiful spots in California. That's why I've stayed. That's why we all live with the risk."

While many residents on Blue Ridge Drive lost everything they own, they still feel fortunate. During the 1982 mudslides, when six homes on the street were destroyed, three residents were killed. But in the earthquake, no residents of the street were injured.

Three people died at the Pacific Garden Mall in collapsed buildings, and the destruction will forever alter the character of downtown Santa Cruz. The open-air mall, a six-block strip of small shops and boutiques bordered by red-tiled walkways and flower beds, had long been the city's unofficial meeting and greeting place, where students, transients and button-down executives mingled in an eclectic pastiche. In a few seconds, the earthquake destroyed the heart of the mall, leaving the strip—which ironically was soon to be honored with a 20th-anniversary celebration—a mass of bricks and glass.

Eleven historic builidngs, many dating from the 1880's, were lost. Almost half of the 600 businesses employing 2,000 people were damaged or destroyed.

"The mall as we knew it is gone," Mayor Mardi Wormhoudt said glumly after surveying the damage.

▲

David King of Santa Cruz waits for friends to help move the last of his possessions from his home of 23 years. King's home near the heavily damaged downtown fell off its foundation. Five days after the quake, he and his parents were still staying at a Red Cross shelter in the civic auditorium.

Photographer:
Bob Carey

◀

President Bush tours the devastated mall in downtown Santa Cruz with local officials. Women in red to left of Bush is Santa Cruz mayor Mardi Wormhoudt.

Photographer:
Bernie Boston

In nearby Watsonville, about 30 buildings—or about one-half of the classic small-town Main Street—will have to be demolished. Also lost is St. Patrick's Church, an immense red-brick building with a 60-foot-tall steeple that has dominated the downtown skyline for 86 years.

While more affluent residents in the Santa Cruz Mountains were able to move in with friends or temporarily rent apartments after the earthquake, hundreds of migrant workers in Watsonville remained homeless. Weeks after the earthquake, about 200 people, many of whom worked in the surrounding broccoli and tomato fields, were still living in tents at a city park.

In Los Gatos, a scenic town in the foothills overlooking the Santa Clara Valley, about 35 older homes, many of them beautifully restored Victorians with ornate gabled roofs, have been condemned.

While many residents busied themselves after the quake negotiating with contractors and structural engineers, Nicki Camp stayed at a homeless shelter and tried to decide how to rebuild her life. Her home in the mountains above Felton had toppled halfway down a ravine and was suspended only by a few redwood trees.

Camp knows she will never recover her old photographs, antique furniture and fine china. But every day after the earthquake, what she thought about most was a small blue crystal perfume bottle—a 25th anniversary present from her husband—and how it glittered when the sunlight streamed through the windows in the late afternoon.

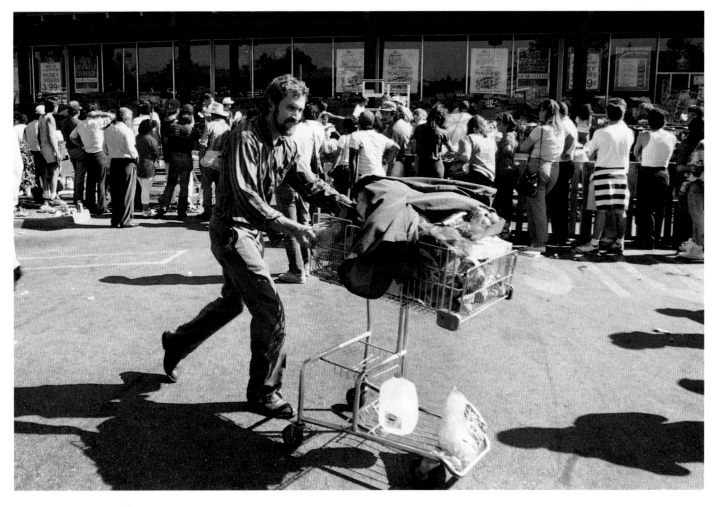

There was a run on supplies in much of Santa Cruz, which was cut off from highway contact with the Bay Area by landslides and collapsed bridges.

Photographer:
Anacleto Rapping

Hours after the quake, a worker looks up at the damaged International Order of Odd Fellows building in Hollister.

Photographer:
Bob Carey

●

Wreckage of a house that crumbled
in Boulder Creek, one of several
devastated towns in the Santa Cruz
Mountains.

Photographer:
Jim Mendenhall

▶

Freda and John Tranbarger perch
on the edge of a 15-foot-deep
fissure that opened in their yard in
Loma Prieta, a Santa Cruz Mountain
town near the epicenter. The crack
was 6 feet wide and 1,000 feet long.
"You should put up a fence and
charge admission," one curious
spectator told them.

Photographer:
Bob Carey

▲

Robin Clayton and her husband, Ray, had recently moved into their house in a quaint section of Los Gatos. The city's older, classic homes were ravaged. The Claytons' house, which cost $750,000, was knocked akilter by the quake. They had a big mortgage and no earth-quake insurance.

Photographer:
Bob Carey

Park in the center of downtown Watsonville was a place for families forced out of their homes to gather, exchange information, look for loved ones, and try to arrange for food or shelter.

Photographer:
Anacleto Rapping

▼

Evacuees at a tent village on the
football field of Watsonville High
School reach for fruit juice
delivered by a utility worker. Some
families spent a week or more in
homeless camps around the city.

Photographer:
Jim Mendenhall

Families forced out of their homes took refuge on the athletic field at Watsonville High School. Consuelo Diaz, seated at right, joins her family around a barbecue in a tent village on the field.

Photographer:
Jim Mendenhall

Woman prepares a meal for her
family in a Watsonville tent
encampment.

Photographer:
Bob Carey

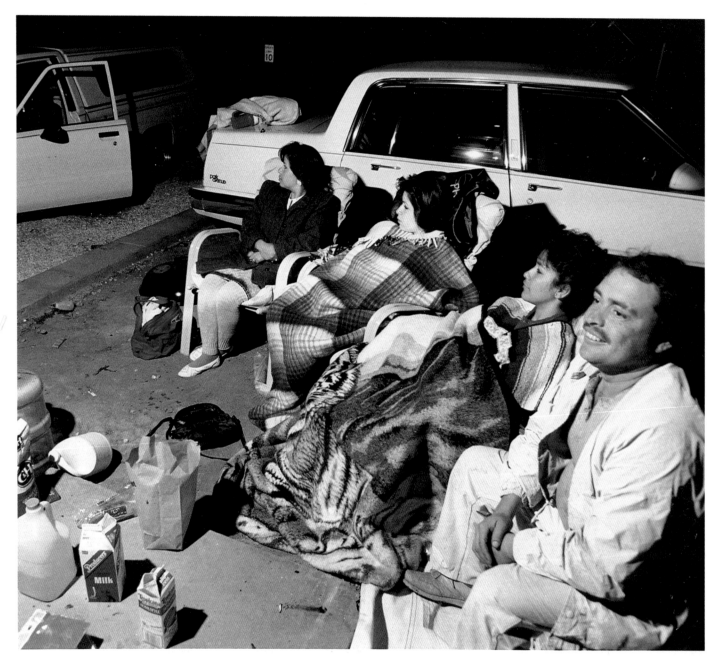

Family made homeless by the quake camps out in Watsonville.

Photographer:
Bob Carey

⬛

Guadalupe Alvarez wipes away tears during a service the Sunday after at St. Patrick's Catholic Church in Watsonville. The landmark church faced probable demolition.

Photographer:
Bob Carey

⬛

In Watsonville, the landmark St. Patrick's Catholic Church, a red-brick building downtown, was damaged. Officials fear it may have to be demolished.

Photographer:
Bob Carey

Myra Casteneda looks from under
her tent in Watsonville. Tent en-
campments sprouted in parks and
the high school field in the Santa
Cruz County town.

Photographer:
Bob Carey

Hotel Cominos, a Salinas landmark famous as a haunt of writer John Steinbeck, was dismantled over the objections of local historians.

Photographer:
Bob Carey

◄

Clock on the landmark Ferry Building at the San Francisco Embarcadero stopped when the quake struck. The flagpole atop the tower also was bent.

Photographer:
Anne Dowie

The Spirit to Carry On

John Balzar

Have you seen what an earthquake does inside a house?" asked Sondra de Roulet as she sat on her front step.

Actually, devastation around her Marina District home was visible everywhere. We had seen plenty already. Apartment buildings crushed into match sticks. Walls of houses thrust at crazy and sickening angles. Broken glass and broken concrete, not to mention broken hearts. We had seen a lot already by walking past the police lines into the danger zone that had been one of America's prized neighborhoods.

"No, I mean inside," she said.

Like others who survived, de Roulet did not want to be alone.

So she invited a reporter and a visiting politician—total strangers—to look inside. Before her nightmare is really over, maybe a year will lapse and there will be a parade of strangers passing through here—insurance adjusters, engineers, inspectors, carpenters, plasterers, painters, utility repairmen, decorators.

Her front door could not be opened. As the landfill on San Francisco's Marina District was whipped to something like the texture of peanut butter by the vibrations of the temblor, the weight of the two-story de Roulet house shifted heavily to the front. The door was compressed into its frame and was now part of the load-bearing front wall.

We entered from the side, through the garage.

The grandfather clock had been sent skidding onto its face. It had kept good time. The hands were frozen at 5:04. The staircase was twisted. Looking down the hall, all of the doorways were drunkenly out of alignment. Those weren't spider webs on the walls, on the ceilings and in the corners. Cracks.

Over each doorway, the beams were shifted and the walls opened into still larger fractures, some an inch wide. Furniture was heaved around the room, scratched and sprung. Some pieces, though, including a 5-foot-high bookshelf, stood untouched, eerie evidence of the capriciousness of earthquakes.

Since the quake, there had been no heat in her house, and no prospect of getting any before the winter storms. No natural gas, either. It took days before the electric power came on—and 10 days before she could rig a standby electric water heater.

She needed a pass to get through the barricades to and from the neighborhood. There was a long waiting list to get an engineer to inspect her dwelling. It would be weeks before contractors could begin repairs.

And then how long would the repairs take? What hidden damage would they find when they peel back the plaster and look at the skeleton of the house?

Meanwhile, it was hard to escape the fear.

Little noises made hearts flop. Sleep was tenuous. Experts warned of deep and long-lasting anxiety, of irritability, of ragged nerves. Eyes told of exhaustion.

But Sondra de Roulet smiled in the face of it.

She was one of the lucky ones. She survived with her family and her spirit and a sort-of house that used to be a home.

Just down the street was worse. Across the bay was worse. South to Santa Cruz was worse.

The quake of October 17, 1989, killed 65.

The good news, this is fewer than first thought.

Injured were 3,089.

The bad news is that property damage was enormous. Officials made only preliminary calculations and were ready to call it the nation's most expensive disaster.

California's Office of Emergency Services two weeks after the quake delivered this grim accounting of damage estimates, approaching $7 billion.

Damage to homes and buildings:

Alameda County, $1,479,104,500
Contra Costa County, $25,000,000
Monterey County, $108,000,000
San Benito County, $103,550,000
San Francisco County, $2,000,000,000
San Mateo County, $292,941,001
Santa Clara County, $727,700,000
Santa Cruz County, $1,526,000,000

Add to that damage to state bridges and roads of $500 million to $1 billion, and to state government buildings of $20 million.

People displaced from their homes, 13,892.

Two weeks after the quake, 29,999 people filed applications for disaster relief.

The quake was felt from the northern reaches of the San Fernando Valley in Los Angeles to southern Oregon. Damage to structures was reported as far south as the uppermost portion of San Luis Obispo County and north to Marin County, a span of 200 miles. And damage

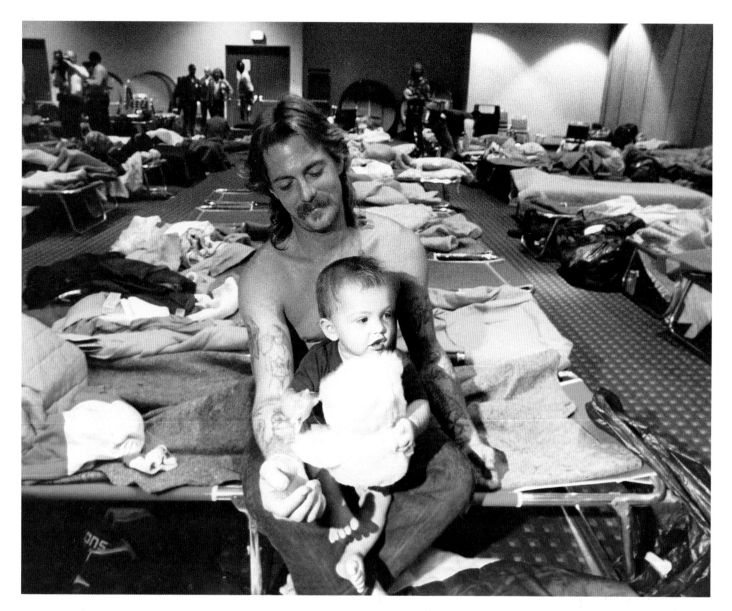

Jamie Lynn Paz, one-year-old, sits on the lap of his mother's friend, Randy Putnam, on the first weekend after the quake. They were among several hundred of the San Francisco homeless who were moved onto cots inside the city's George Moscone Center. The large convention center south of Market Street was the main relief center in the city for homeless street people.

Photographer:
Bob Durell

East Bay commuters leave special ferry brought to the Bay Area from Los Angeles, where it normally carries visitors to Santa Catalina Island. Extra ferries were needed to help commuters into San Francisco left stranded by closure of the Bay Bridge. This was Monday, Oct. 23, when a heavy rain and wind storm made commuting a horror.

Photographer:
Tom Kelsey

reached another 60 miles inland in the Sacramento-San Joaquin delta region.

There is an emotional toll too. The quake's horrifying images now become deeply unsettling memories to gnaw at everyone in earthquake country:

A freeway collapsing. High in the air, a bridge span hinging open. Cutting through a dead woman to reach a live boy. The Marina District couple found dead, under a collapsed doorway, locked in a final embrace. Friends and family shouting the name of a child missing in the rubble of a Santa Cruz shopping center, hoping vainly the youngster would be alive and know she was not forgotten.

The hardships of the aftermath are as impossible to measure as they are impossible to ignore:

A weekly newspaper in Santa Cruz folds. The Fisherman's Wharf Association worries that half of the 30,000 workers in San Francisco's tourist mecca may be laid off for lack of business, just as the holidays approach. The Moss Landing Marine Laboratory in Monterey is a total loss. Merle Byrd's small house in Los Gatos survived the giant 1906 quake, but not this one. Millions upon millions of agonies, big and small.

But once knocked down, the Bay Area did not stay down.

Not for a minute.

Forget all the cliches of how Californians are incurably selfish, and that nothing around us seems to work anymore.

That changed in 15 seconds.

Barely had the shaking stopped, and people dusted themselves off and started pulling together. Citizens directed traffic. Crime went down. Government's emergency plans, while not perfect, were not wanting either. Politicians, or at least most of them, looked more like leaders. Food, money, volunteers, sympathy and support poured in. A masseuse gave free rubdowns for weary police; the ultra-posh Stanford Court put up some homeless people in five-star fashion.

You hardly heard the word no.

The Bay Area's first World Series became baseball's oddest—two weeks, four games, no champagne. But, yes, the game did go on.

In one of America's premier convention towns, a cheer went up when the American Association for Marriage and Family Therapy said yes, and went ahead with its convention eight days after the earthquake. Some found the theme fitting: building bridges, creating balance.

With a makeshift fleet of ferry boats, its modern BART trains and compound ingenuity, the congested Bay Area managed, yes, to avoid commuter gridlock. A story was told of the two motorists who met on a darkened road after the quake. The pavement was ruptured and neither could get home in the emergency. So they traded names, phone numbers and drove off in each other's car.

Along with everything else, the mighty shift of the continental plates had brought forth spirit. Individual spirit, civic spirit, can-do spirit.

The spirit to carry on.

ACKNOWLEDGMENTS

The following contributed to Los Angeles Times coverage of the Bay Area Earthquake

Editor Shelby Coffey III; Managing Editor George Cotliar; Metropolitan Editor Craig Turner; Assistant Managing Editor Terry Schwadron; Earthquake Assignment Desk: W.B. Rood, Tim Reiterman, Roxane Arnold, Cynthia Craft, Max Vanzi, Joel Greenberg, Julie Wilson; Special Section Editors: Peter H. King, Stan Burroway, John Cherwa, Robert Magnuson, Patrick McMahon, John Brownell; News Editors: James Bornemeier, Rick Collins, Gary Metzker; Photo Editors: Larry Armstrong, Bob Chamberlin, Cindy Hively, Con Keyes, Tammy Lechner, Jerome McClendon, Marsha Traeger, Mike Zacchino

In San Francisco: Philip Hager, Dan Morain, Victor Zonana, Norma Kaufman, John Balzar, Edwin Chen, Warwick Elston, Lily Eng, Larry Green, Martha Groves, Ron Harris, Nancy Hill-Holtzman, Robert L. Jackson, Robert A. Jones, Tamara Jones, J. Michael Kennedy, Jim Murray, Dean Murphy, Ross Newhan, Jim Newton, Suzette Parmley, Mike Penner, Louis Sahagun, Janny Scott, Ronald L. Soble, Larry Stewart, George Stein

In Oakland: Stephanie Chavez, Ashley Dunn, Andrea Ford, Kenneth J. Garcia, Paul Jacobs, Maria L. La Ganga, David Lauter, Scott Masko, Maria Newman, Richard C. Paddock, George Ramos, Douglas Shuit, Sheryl Stolberg, Donna K.H. Walters, Tracy Wilkinson

In Santa Cruz and Santa Clara counties: Eric Bailey, Jack Cheevers, Miles Corwin, Michele Fuetsch, Scott Harris, Marita Hernandez, Charles Hillinger, Tracey Kaplan, Thomas H. Maugh II, Ed Newton, Richard O'Reilly, Hector Tobar

In Sacramento: George Skelton, Virginia Ellis, Jerry Gillam, John Hurst, Carl Ingram, William Trombley, Daniel M. Weintraub, Patti Cole

In Los Angeles: Harry Anderson, Jim Bates, John Chandler, Russell Chandler, Steve Chawkins, Steven R. Churm, Frank Clifford, Richard Lee Colvin, Rich Connell, Michael Connelly, John Dart, Tina Daunt, Cathleen Decker, Maura Dolan, Paul Feldman, David Ferrell, Jane Fritsch, Gabe Fuentes, Mary Lou Fulton, Tom Furlong, Denise Gellene, John Glionna, Larry Gordon, Nieson Himmel, Jeffrey Kaye, Bruce Keppel, Carla Lazzareschi, Patrick Lee, Keith Love, Eric Malnic, Lee Margulies, Penelope McMillan, Richard Meyer, Joanna Miller, Myrna Oliver, Steve Padilla, Judy Pasternak, Jonathan Peterson, Kenneth Reich, William Rempel, Anne C. Roark, Kevin Roderick, Sebastian Rotella, David Savage, Jesus Sanchez, Bob Schwartz, Bob Secter, Jube Shiver, Larry B. Stammer, Jill Stewart, Ronald B. Taylor, Lois Timnick, Jenifer Warren, Dan Weikel, Robert Welkos, Linda Williams, Elaine Woo, Nancy Yoshihara, Greg Beckman, Pat Benson, Tom Bronzini, Tom Durkin, Jane Engle, Gary Fong, Robert Harlow, Mary Ann Hoffarth, Fred Holley, James Houston, Burt Irwin, DeWayne Johnson, Raymond Johnson, Bill Kershaw, Phillip Krapf, Jim Marnel, Bruce McLeod, Al Perrin, Larry Snipes, Clark Stevens, Walt Taylor, Paul Whitefield, Waren Wolfswinkel, Martin Zimmerman

In San Diego: Greg Johnson

In New York: John Goldman

In Washington: Kevin Davis, Sam Fullwood III, Doyle McManus, Michael Ross

Newspaper Graphics: Tom Trapnell, David Puckett, Marty Steffens

Research: Lilia Beebe, Jim Cady, Kristin Christopher, Lauri Ferguson, Kevin H. Fox, William Holmes, Tom Lutgen, Cecilia Rasmussen, Greg Rice, Peter Johnson, Tracy Thomas, Nona Yates

Photographers: Lori Shepler, Gary Friedman, Bernie Boston, Tom Kelsey, Jayne Kamin-Oncea, Ken Lubas, Bob Durell, Anne Dowie, Jim Mendenhall, J. Albert Diaz, Bob Carey, Anacleto Rapping, Larry Davis, James Pease, Joe Kennedy